Rookie
Talk About It™

Perseverance:
I Have Grit!

by Jodie Shepherd

Content Consultant

Samantha Gambino, Psy.D.
Licensed Psychologist, New York, New York

Reading Consultant

Jeanne M. Clidas, Ph.D.
Reading Specialist

Children's Press®
An Imprint of Scholastic Inc.

Library of Congress Cataloging-in-Publication Data
Shepherd, Jodie, author.
  Perseverance : I have grit / by Jodie Shepherd.
      pages cm. -- (Rookie talk about it)
  Summary: "Teaches the reader about perseverance."-- Provided by publisher.
  ISBN 978-0-531-21511-1 (library binding) -- ISBN 978-0-531-21379-7 (pbk.)
1. Perseverance (Ethics)--Juvenile literature. 2. Conduct of life--Juvenile literature.
3. Success in children--Juvenile literature. I. Title.

  BJ1533.P4S54 2016
  179.9--dc23   2015018083

Produced by Spooky Cheetah Press
Design by Keith Plechaty

Printed in China 62

SCHOLASTIC, CHILDREN'S PRESS, ROOKIE TALK ABOUT IT™, and associated logos are trademarks and/or registered trademarks of Scholastic Inc.

1 2 3 4 5 6 7 8 9 10 R 25 24 23 22 21 20 19 18 17 16

Table of Contents

What Is Grit?

Imagine you want to get really good at dribbling a basketball. But you keep messing up. What would someone with grit do?

Grit is another word for *perseverance*. That means you have the courage and toughness to stick with something. Want some examples? There are many people you have probably heard of who had to show lots of grit to succeed.

Try, Try Again!

Jane Goodall studied chimpanzees for more than 50 years. Her many discoveries made her famous.

At first, the chimps would not let Goodall near them. She was **frustrated**. She needed to study the animals up close.

For Goodall, failure was not an option! It took a year of trying, but she finally got the chimpanzees to trust her.

Think of something new you learned to do in the last year. Did you do it perfectly the first time you tried? Probably not. It is exciting to learn something new. But it takes patience. It takes practice. It takes time.

11

To persevere, you take one small step at a time. You did not learn to ride a two-wheeler all at once. Maybe you started with a tricycle. Then training wheels helped you balance. Finally, one day you rode a bike all by yourself!

Make a paper perseverance chain. Each time you work on your goal, make another link from colored construction paper. Attach it to your chain. When you succeed, hang it up for everyone to see!

Do Not Be Afraid to Fail

If you cannot do something the first time you try, that is okay. Failing is a good way to learn.

Orville and Wilbur Wright were **pioneers**. They made history when they flew their airplane back in 1903. But they had failed many times first. The Wright brothers learned from their mistakes. After each failure, the next plane was better.

The Wright brothers made the first-ever successful flight.

We all fail sometimes. And sometimes it gets us down. When you become frustrated, tell yourself, "I know I can do this."

Remember, even if you fail sometimes, you are still learning. You are getting a little better every time you try again. Getting to your goal is great. But simply trying is also very important.

Fighting Frustration

Martin Luther King Jr. worked his whole life to change laws that were unfair to African Americans. He believed all people should have the same rights, no matter the color of their skin. King tried to change people's minds with **nonviolent** protests. Change came very slowly, but King never lost hope. He worked for many years before these laws were changed.

Dr. King spoke about his long fight for equal rights. He said: "If you can't fly, run; if you can't run, walk; if you can't walk, crawl; but by all means keep moving."

Sometimes it is hard work to persevere. You may feel frustrated. You may feel you will never get to your goal. Be **resilient**, like Dr. King! Get up, brush yourself off, and try again.

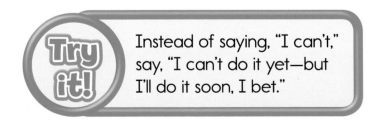

Instead of saying, "I can't," say, "I can't do it yet—but I'll do it soon, I bet."

You Have Grit!

Once you have achieved your goal, give yourself a pat on the back. You persevered. You did it! Take some time to feel proud. Then find a new challenge to work toward!

Malala Yousafzai

Malala was born on July 12, 1997, in the country of Pakistan. Some people in Pakistan did not believe girls should be allowed to go to school. Eleven-year-old Malala did not agree. She bravely spoke out, even though people threatened her. She went to school and encouraged other girls to do the same.

On October 9, 2012, Malala was shot by people who disagreed with her. When she got out of the hospital, she continued to speak out for girls' education. She persevered. And the world listened. In 2014, Malala was awarded the Nobel Peace Prize. She is the youngest person ever to receive that honor.

It Starts with You!

Increase your powers of perseverance! Here's how:

1. **Make a goal.** Then think of the steps you will need to take to get to your goal. Make a checklist so you can cross off each step as you accomplish it.

2. **Use your imagination.** Make a picture in your head of how you will feel when you reach your goal. Let that motivate you.

3. **Practice, practice, practice.** Stick with it a little longer every time you work at your goal.

Read the story below and imagine what you might do in this situation.

You have been trying to learn a new song for weeks. But you keep hitting the wrong notes every time you practice. What should you do?

Need help getting started?

- What can you say to yourself to boost your confidence?

- Think about Jane Goodall, the Wright brothers, and Martin Luther King Jr. What would they do?

- How will you feel once you have learned to play the song perfectly?

Do You Have Grit?

1. I always want to play or compete, even if I think I am going to lose.

☐ True ☐ False

2. I would rather try something hard even if I cannot do it well than succeed at something easy.

☐ True ☐ False

3. I do not feel bad about myself when I fail at something. I tell myself I will do better next time.

☐ True ☐ False

4. If I cannot do something well right away, I keep trying.

☐ True ☐ False

If you answered mostly with Trues, you are on your way to becoming a perseverance superstar! If you answered mostly with Falses, try to remember that not succeeding just means you need to keep trying!

Glossary

frustrated (FRUHSS-trayt-ed): feeling helpless or discouraged

nonviolent (non-VYE-lent): peaceful; not using physical force

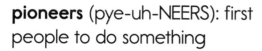

pioneers (pye-uh-NEERS): first people to do something

resilient (rih-ZIL-yuhnt): able to bounce back and succeed after facing something difficult

Index

Facts for Now

Visit this Scholastic Web site for more information on perseverance:
www.factsfornow.scholastic.com
Enter the keyword **Perseverance**

About the Author

Jodie Shepherd, who also writes under the name Leslie Kimmelman, is an award-winning author of dozens of books for children, both fiction and nonfiction. She is a children's book editor, too.